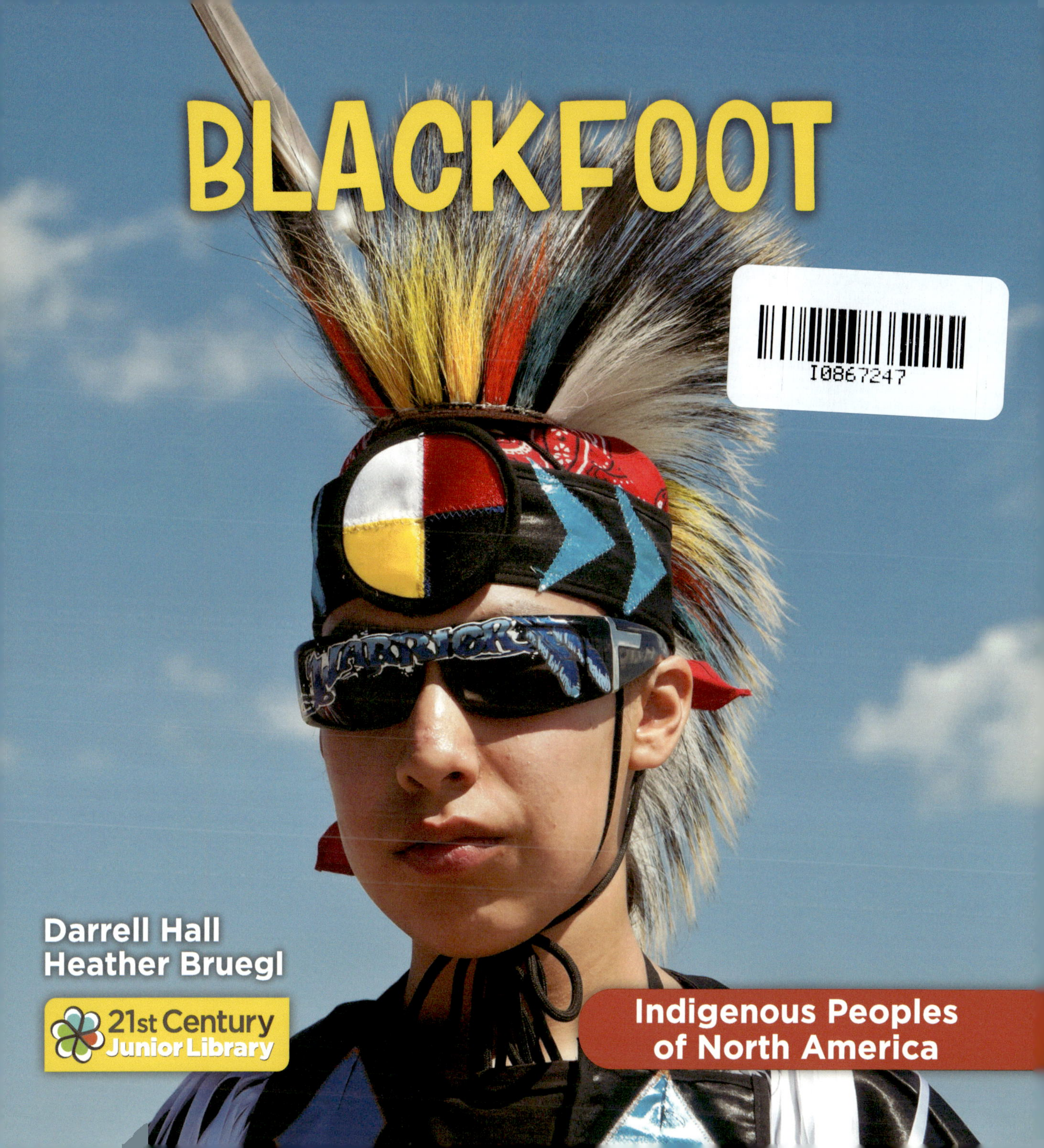

BLACKFOOT

Darrell Hall
Heather Bruegl

21st Century Junior Library

Indigenous Peoples of North America

Published in the United States of America by:

CHERRY LAKE PRESS
2395 South Huron Parkway, Suite 200, Ann Arbor, Michigan 48104
www.cherrylakepress.com

Reading Adviser: Beth Walker Gambro, MS, Ed., Reading Consultant, Yorkville, IL

Photo Credits: © Michelle Gilder/Alamy, cover, title page, 5; © Oasisamuel/Dreamstime.com, 6; © AP Photo/David Goldman, file, 8; © Darrell Hall, 9; © Greg Lindstrom /Flathead Beacon via AP, 10–11; © Frank Sun, CC BY-SA 4.0 via Wikimedia Commons, 12; © David P. Lewis/Shutterstock, 14; © Jeff McIntosh/The Canadian Press via AP, 17; © Rick Rudnicki/Alamy, 18–19; © AP Photo/ The Independent Record, Eliza Wiley, 21

Cherry Lake Press is an imprint of Cherry Lake Publishing Group.

Library of Congress Cataloging-in-Publication Data has been filed and is available at catalog.loc.gov

Cherry Lake Publishing Group would like to acknowledge the work of the Partnership for 21st Century Learning, a Network of Battelle for Kids. Please visit Battelle for Kids online for more information.

Printed in the United States of America

Note from publisher: Websites change regularly, and their future contents are outside of our control. Supervise children when conducting any recommended online searches for extended learning opportunities.

CHERRY LAKE PRESS

CONTENTS

Who We Are 4

Our Lives Today 10

Our Ancestral Lands 15

Carrying Traditions Forward 18

Glossary 22

Find Out More 23

Index 24

About the Authors 24

WHO WE ARE

The Blackfoot are Indigenous peoples. They call themselves *Niitsitapi*. It means "the original people." They were created from the land that they live on. They and their **ancestors** have lived in what is now North America for more than 18,000 years. That is thousands of years before the end of the last Ice Age.

Four Blackfoot nations make up the Blackfoot **Confederacy**. They are Kainai Nation (Blood Tribe), Siksika Nation (Blackfoot), Piikani Nation (North Peigan), and Amskapi Pikuni (Blackfeet Nation). Most of the Blackfoot Confederacy is in Alberta, Canada. Amskapi Pikuni is mostly in Montana in the United States.

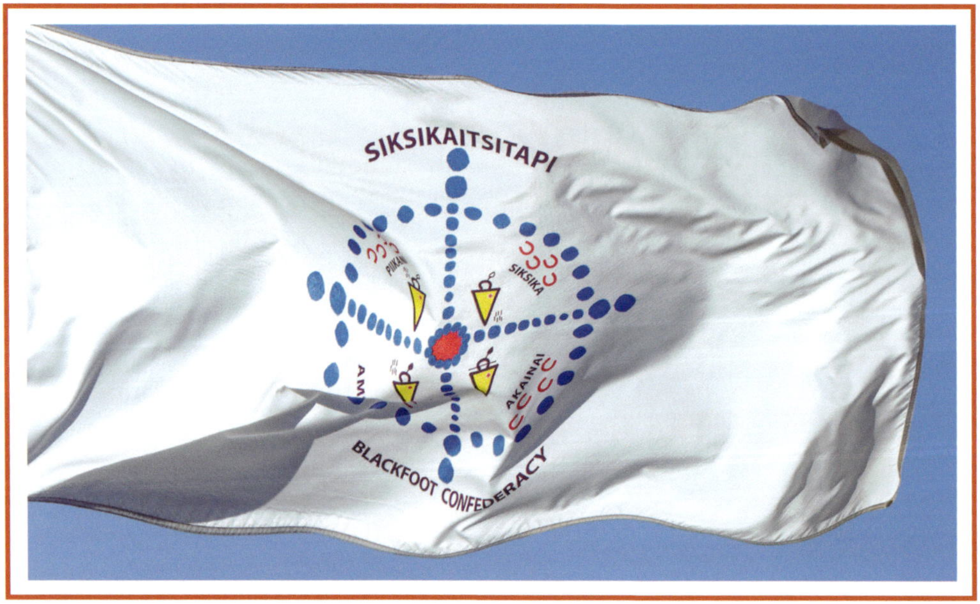

Think!

How do you think having parts of the confederacy in different countries affects Blackfoot peoples?

Ceremony, family, and community are important to the Blackfoot people. their ceremonies and language are the main part of their identity. The Blackfoot people are connected to the land through the songs and **sacred bundles** given to them by the animals.

The Blackfoot people value **kinship** deeply. They are part of age grade societies, or groups of people around the same age. They are taught about life and the environment in these groups. Members move through the stages of life together.

They have important responsibilities. They take care of their people through ceremony, songs, and prayer.

The Blackfoot are land keepers. They believe in being **stewards** for all living things. They seek to live and work in harmony with the land. They promote new growth through land management. They practice **controlled burns**. Long ago, ground blackened by these fires would turn the bottoms of their **moccasins** black. This is why they became known as Blackfoot.

Shield Keepers and Chief Mountain Guardians such as those shown here work to protect Blackfeet Nation land and culture.

OUR LIVES TODAY

In Canada, Blackfoot nations are located in Alberta. There are around 25,000 Blackfoot citizens in Canada. The Blackfeet Nation in the United States is in Montana. It is home to over 17,000 Blackfeet citizens.

Individual Blackfoot citizens live across North America and even around the world. Many serve or have served overseas in the Canadian or U.S. military. Blackfoot people are very educated. They have many different kinds of professions, such as teachers, actors, authors, and historians.

Jesse DesRosier is a Blackfeet veteran of the U.S. Marine Corps and language teacher.

Actress Lily Gladstone

Lily Gladstone is a famous actress. She grew up in Blackfeet Nation in Montana. She starred in the 2023 movie *Killers of the Flower Moon*. She won a Golden Globe and was nominated for an Academy Award. She was the first Indigenous woman to do so.

Stephen Graham Jones is an award-winning *New York Times* best-selling author. He is a citizen of Blackfeet Nation but grew up in Texas.

Dr. Michael Bruised Head, or Ninna Piiksii (Chief Bird), is a Blackfoot elder and cultural teacher. He is from the Blood Reserve of the Kainai First Nation. Dr. Bruised Head is working to bring Indigenous place names back to national parks and other places.

Blackfoot people in both the United States and Canada are active and vital parts of their communities and economies. Many are focused on restoring their language and caring for the land.

Make a Guess!

Why do you think people are working to bring back Indigenous place names? Why is it important?

Áísínai'pi (Writing-On-Stone) Provincial Park in Alberta, Canada, is at the center of Blackfoot ancestral lands.

OUR ANCESTRAL LANDS

The **ancestral** lands of the Blackfoot Confederacy stretched from central Alberta to all of Montana and into Wyoming. They spread from the eastern Rocky Mountains into the Great Plains. These lands were the Blackfoot's to protect and care for.

Look!

Look at the picture of Blackfoot lands on the opposite page. What do you see? What do you think the climate is like?

The Blackfoot traveled these lands throughout the year. They lived a **nomadic** lifestyle. The American bison, or buffalo, was essential. The Blackfoot hunted it for food, hides, and bones. Women in the tribe processed the bison hides. The Blackfoot people lived in **tipis** made from the hides. These tipis could be put up and taken down for traveling. The nations moved as the seasons changed and bison herds moved.

Living and moving with the rhythm of seasons, the Blackfoot have a spiritual relationship with the land. But government policies forced Blackfoot nations onto **reserves** and **reservations** in Canada and the United States.

Piikani Nation Chief Stan Grier signs a declaration against a planned oil pipeline in Canada.

Blackfoot life changed. Blackfoot nations could not move freely across the land. Many of their traditions and cultural practices were outlawed by federal governments.

The Blackfoot people's relationship with the land is still strong. They carry it with them and continue to work for change and the restoration of their ancestral land.

CARRYING TRADITIONS FORWARD

Today, Blackfoot citizens continue their traditions. They are working to build a strong future for the next generations. Every year, Blackfoot nations gather for 4-day Indian Days celebrations. They enjoy powwows, Indian relay horse racing, rodeos, and golfing. They celebrate who they are by singing, dancing, and sharing food. The dancers compete for prize money in different style dance competitions with their **regalia**.

Create!

Research a style of dance performed at Blackfoot powwows. Create a poster display that tells about the history of the dance, the regalia that is worn, and how dancers are judged.

The Kainai Nation is bringing fire guardians back to their prairie homeland. Fire guardians are responsible for caring for the land with controlled burns. Controlled burns prevent wildfires. They also help get rid of **invasive species** and help plants such as berry bushes grow strong.

Blackfoot peoples in both countries are working to restore the bison population. Bison are a **keystone species**. U.S. anti-Indigenous policies had bison herds killed to weaken Indigenous nations. Bison nearly went extinct.

Ask Questions!

What else do you want to know about Blackfoot traditions today? How can you find answers to your questions?

Canadian policies used the falling bison population to force Blackfoot nations onto reserves. Today, the bison population is returning. Bison herds can now be found in places they haven't been for 150 years.

Caring for the land and passing on traditions helps build a strong future for Blackfoot people.

GLOSSARY

ancestors (AN-seh-sterz) past generations of a family or cultural group

ancestral (an-SEH-struhl) belonging to past generations of a family or cultural group

confederacy (kuhn-FED-er-uh-see) a group of nations with official alliances and shared decision making

controlled burns (kuhn-TROHLD BERNZ) planned fires that help prevent forest fires and keep the land healthy

invasive species (in-VAY-siv SPEE-sheez) non-native species that enter an environment by force or by accident and spread quickly

keystone species (KEE-stohn SPEE-sheez) wildlife that have a big impact on their entire ecosystem

kinship (KIN-ship) family relationships

moccasins (MAHK-uh-sinz) soft shoes made out of animal hide

nomadic (noh-MA-dik) describing people who move from place to place

regalia (rih-GAYL-yuh) fine clothing; often ceremonial

reservations (reh-zer-VAY-shuhnz) legally designated plots of land held in trust for Indigenous peoples by the U.S. federal government

reserves (rih-ZERVZ) legally designated areas of land for Indigenous peoples in Canada

sacred bundles (SAY-kruhd BUN-duhlz) holy objects central to Blackfoot beliefs and ceremonies

stewards (STOO-erdz) caretakers

tipis (TEE-peez) traditional Indigenous tent dwellings made of animal skins

FIND OUT MORE

Books

King, Thomas, and Natasha Donovan. *Borders.* New York, NY: Little, Brown and Company, 2021.

Sorell, Traci. *We Are Still Here! Native American Truths Everyone Should Know.* Watertown, MA: Charlesbridge, 2021.

Online

With an adult, explore more online with these suggested searches.

- "Our Lands & Tribes," Siksikaitsitapi Blackfoot Confederacy
- "The Story of the Blackfoot People," Virtual Exhibit, Glenbow Museum

Say Hello!

Oki (OH-kee) is a way to say "hi" in the Blackfoot language.

INDEX

activism, 17, 21
American communities, 4, 6-7, 10, 15, 16-17, 18, 20
ancestral lands, 13, 14-17, 20-21
art and artists, 7

bison, 16, 20-21
Blackfoot Confederacy, 6-7, 20

Canadian communities, 4, 6, 7, 10, 14-15, 16-17, 21
controlled burns, 8, 20

dance, 7, 18

environmental stewardship, 8-9, 13, 15, 16, 17, 20-21

games and sports, 18-19
Gladstone, Lily, 12

history of the Blackfoot, 4-8, 13, 14-17, 20-21

Indigenous place names, 13, 14
Indigenous rights, 16-17

lands, 8-9, 13, 14-17, 20-21
language, 4, 7, 13

modern life, 8-9, 10-13, 17, 18-21

nomadism, 16-17

professions, 9, 10-13, 20

reservations and reserves, 10, 16-17, 18, 21

traditions, 7, 13, 16-17, 18-21
tribal leaders, 17

veterans, 10-11

ABOUT THE AUTHORS

Darrell Hall was born and raised on the Blackfeet reservation as an outdoors man, rancher, and horseman. His Blackfoot name is Spoo-Mok-ii-Tok, meaning "Helping Rock." He was the leader of the Brave Dog Society in Amskapi Pikuni for 10 years and has helped all societies and Medicine bundles since he was a young man. His latest work was as a Chief Mountain Guardian Shield Keeper. They implemented Blackfoot culture into environmental work and brought the culture to their people to help in bringing back their identity as Niisitapii.

Heather Bruegl, a member of the Oneida Nation of Wisconsin/Stockbridge-Munsee, is a public historian and educator. Her Munsee name is Kiishookunkwe, meaning "Sunflower in Full Bloom."